The Tantra of Prosperity:

Unlocking Your True Wealth

I0088596

With Tricia Fiske & Laurie LaMantia

Copyright © 2021 Laurie LaMantia. & Tricia Fiske

LALA Unlimited 154 Easy Street Carol Stream, IL 60188 847.640.8923 LALA Unlimited

All rights reserved. No part of this book may be reproduced, stored, or transmitted by any means—whether auditory, graphic, mechanical, or electronic—without written permission of the author, except in the case of brief excerpts used in critical articles and reviews. Unauthorized reproduction of any part of this work is illegal and is punishable by law.

The authors of this book does not dispense financial advice or prescribe the use of any technique as a form of financial and money investing as a financial advisor and planner would do. The intent of the author is only to offer information of a general nature to help the reader in their quest for emotional and spiritual well-being. In the event the reader uses any of the information in this book for themselves, which is their constitutional right, the author and/or publisher assume no responsibility for their actions.

This book is a work of non-fiction. Unless otherwise noted, the author and the publisher make no explicit guarantees as to the accuracy of the information contained in this book and in some cases, names of people and places have been altered to protect their privacy.

ISBN 978-1-944923-07-5 (softcover)

In Appreciation

As with all projects of passion and inspiration – there are many who come together to make the dream a reality.

First, we would like to thank Yogarupa Rod Stryker for his unending desire and ability to share the divine teachings of Tantra to thousands of students around the world. It was his program, **Tantra Shakti**: The Power and Radiant Soul of Yoga (see www.parayoga.com) that inspired this project...thank you Yogorupa!

We would like to thank the generous time and talented contribution of Kathryn Carr, who is featured in the asana video practices. You are a powerful yoga teacher and wonderful yoga practicioner. Thank you for sharing yourself through the asana practices.

The introduction music of the meditations and asanas were record and shared by Sylviane Conzen an inspired musician and artist – thank you!

Contents

INTRODUCTION

What is this program about?

- You becoming a powerful energy investor.

- Using the energy creating principles of Tantra to awaken, direct and focus (a.k.a invest) your energy into the wealth you desire – and to re-member that it is already present.

- Learning to invest your attention and energy consciously and transition from poverty to prosperity, worry to wealth, limitation to abundance, and efforting to ease.

The Program

- Session 1 - PREPARE - bring your energy in readyment for this prosperi-ty work
- Session 2 - CALM - all is well, you are safe relax into the grace of life
- Session 3 - AWAKEN (solar) - to the inherent prosperity of life and to you are a wealthy energy presence
- Session 4 - ALCHEMIZE (fire) - scarcity and limitation
- Session 5 - ALIGN - (chakra alignment) for prosperity to flow
- Session 6 - ATTRACT - you are already that which you seek
- Session 7 - ALLOW - allow prosperity
- Session 8 - FLOW - your worthiness is never in doubt

8 sessions include:

- The session _intention_, overview and _teaching_

- _Asana_ yoga practice that teaches the energetic essence of the teaching

- Breath work, _pranayama_, that embeds the energetic intention into your pranic field

- Journal work – to help integrate the mind/body consciousness of the session

- Meditation – to unlock the unlimited potential of the session

Objectives – what you will learn

1. The power that you have to be a conscious prosperity creator

2. Tools that will help you mobilize and direct your energy towards prosperity, wealth and abundance.

3. Clarity about where you have been limiting yourself

4. The ability to focus your energy into prosperity.

5. Acknowledgement that Wealth energy is always flowing and available to you – always and in all ways.

What do we mean by prosperity

- Prosperity is aliveness, abundance, potential, wealth and ever expanding flow of energy.

What do we mean by Tantra

- Tantra is energy flow

    - Energy is awakened and mobilized in the body and consciously directed.

- Tantra and Effortlessness

    - The art of learning flow – non-doing doing – where the dancer becomes the dance, where the creator becomes the creation.

    - Tantra is the awareness and acknowledgment of energy flowing so the creator becomes the creation

    - You the wealth creator becomes wealth

    - Learning the grace of ease

- Earning not needed – allowing the fruits of the divine vine, which is already there & here, wanting to expand

Recommendation for how to use this program

- Set aside 2.5 hours on the same day for the next 8 weeks.

- Try to do the whole session in one segment (around 2 hours). And then wait a week before doing the next session (if possible).

    - Listen to the teaching – then journal.

    - Take a short break.

    - Then do the asana practice, and pranayama

    - Journal your reflections

    - Take a short break

    - Meditate

    - Marinate: take a day or two to let the teaching and practice marinate in your daily life. If you have additional thoughts or feelings – journal them. Maybe re-listen to the teaching and/or redo the practices.

    - Repeat the pranayama and meditation daily until the next week's session.

Recommendation for how to make the most of this program

- Allow yourself the time and space to do this program and process.

- Give yourself permission to allow what comes up – come up and share with you.

- Experience – not just theory – experience the levels of change and awakening – feeling the power and new understandings that come as a part of this program.

- Be open and willing to feel what you feel.

- Realize you are doing deep and powerful energy work to awaken to your natural wealth and prosperity.

- Celebrate and appreciate yourself for doing this work.

- Please give yourself the gift of grace – minimize judgement, righteousness, expectation and perfection

- Don't create your future from your past – let yourself create a new wealth reality from a new energy body.

  - Where you put your attention is what creates your reality

- Remember Ease and Flow is the natural state of wealth and abundance.

Commitment:

I invest my energy into:

- awakening to a new way to look at prosperity and wealth

- allowing my natural prosperity to flow

- embracing my glorious potential

- knowing that I have access to unlimited energy

- remembering who I really am

Yoga Alliance

Tricia Fiske is YACEP (Yoga Alliance Continuing Education Certified). Therefore, once you finish the course you will get 20 hours of continuing education yoga alliance credit hours. 20 YA CECs.

A bit about Tricia Fiske

Tricia, 500 E-RYT, Level 3 ParaYoga Instructor, YACEP, BA, is primary faculty for Prairie Yoga's Foundation and Advanced Teacher Training programs. A leader and major influencer in Chicago's yoga community, she has been studying with ParaYoga founder Yogarupa Rod Stryker since 2000. She recently co-authored the book, **From Alignment to Enlightenment**: *Using Props to Achieve Stability and Ease in Yoga Poses*. Her teaching emphasizes the energetic qualities of asana and the ease, clarity and freedom found in Meditation.

A bit about Laurie LaMantia

Laurie LaMantia is a successful entrepreneur, business professor and yogi who shares her wisdom about developing wealth consciousness to her many students. She is the author of **Effortless Wealth**: *An investment guide for developing your wealth consciousness*. From owning a prospering manufacturing company to teaching Entrepreneurship at DePaul University, she has honed her wealth creating perspective and wishes to share it in the hopes you too will benefit from this expansive understanding about the wealth that is meant for and available to you.

Journal & Reflection   Date:

What do I hope to learn and <u>experience</u> from this program?

What would I love to <u>let go of</u> as a result of this program?

Journal & Reflect

How do I feel about prosperity now? How would I define it? How does money and wealth fit in to my definition?

SESSION 1: PREPARE

PREPARE

PREPARE

Begin to see yourself as an investor – an energy investor

- The power of this program is that you will get to experience yourself as a powerful investor who creates by how you invest your life energy...by how you think and feel. And as you get clearer about where and how you are investing your prana (life-force), the more choice you have about what you truly want to invest in.

- The tantra energy creation and direction tools will enable you to create an abundance of prana ~ life force that you will learn how to invest (sense it, build it, direct it) consciously and wisely - hence the journaling for clarity.

- Therefore, it is powerful to see yourself as an investor – intentionally directing your prana into the wealth and prosperity you desire (*a desire in Sanskrit is a sankalpa*).

- Know – that it is ok to think of yourself as an *investor* – one who knows what they want to invest in and how to invest wisely.

Energy follows thought

- Tantra is a philosophical system that sees the world as sacred and provides a comprehensive science that empowers you to experience it.

- What you think about expands and wherever the mind goes – so goes energy. So, if your energy is scattered or focused on lack, limitation or money worries, your energy will follow and expand those thoughts of limitation.

- The tools of Tantra like pranayama (conscious control of your breath), will help your mind come calm and come under conscious control.

- As Rod Stryker notes in Tantra Shakti "since it is easier to control your breath and energy than it is to control your mind, taking advantage of this relationship (between mind and energy) is a key feature of tantric practice."

Expand your definition of wealth

- When most of us hear the word 'wealth,' we think of money or financial wealth. However, it is helpful to expand our definition of wealth from little "w", which means money and/or finances, to Wealth with a capital "W", as in the huge, unlimited world of abundance and fun that is always flowing as a part of life.

- Think a wealth of opportunity, a wealth of health, a wealth of possibility, a wealth of fun, a wealth of love.

- The unlimited life force known as prana is WEALTH. It is this unseen Wealth-Energy surrounding us always and in all ways. The capitals are reminding us of this Universal-Unseen-Force-of-Aliveness that is flowing around us, to us and through us.

- Looking at Prosperity & Wealth this way will let us grow a general *felt-sense* (feeling in your body and in your mind) of this WUW, Wealth-Unlimited-Wealth, energy – that is around you always. Can you feel how expansive and paradigm shifting this can be?

- **And a big benefit of this new perspective on Wealth is that as we develop our WUW consciousness, our little-wealth money will flow.**

The journey of a soul on earth

- Divinity (you) takes on the illusion of limitation – as part of coming into the body – and then as part of the soul's journeys picks up learnings that shape it and give it certain gifts - as it were – but these are part of the human experience -they do not replace nor are they meant to displace the true Divine Essence that is animating and igniting your body proper.

- As we journey into the prosperity of tantra and the tantra of prosperity – we are learning to emerge the soul from the tight grip of limited mind into its full empowered glory in the body & to embody the perfection that is us in the unique body mind complex.

- Let this time in the tantra of prosperity – allow you to open to the unique divinity that is in you as you. Let your unique prosperity flow through you – from the unlimited Divine, where all things are possible and all things exist – to flow in grace and ease through you and to you – because it is you and you are It.

- Whatever has brought you here – thank it – all that you think is good or bad – does not matter – you are here NOW – and this is a most auspicious moment of integration.

  Thank yourself for being here, appreciate the prosperity of life as it flows through you in this present moment – for in the NOW is where all prosperity and wealth abide. In the NOW of clarity and wakefulness can you experience that which you truly are – magnificent divinity – unlimited prosperity, an eternal Wealth-Spring – walking on 2 legs – how amazing!

Wealth can be effortless

- Most of us have an unconscious, unquestioned assumption that there has to be a great deal of effort, a.k.a., hard work in creating wealth because it is hard to come by, and that we need to be deserving of wealth.

- Tantra helps us expand our view of the world and ourselves. It helps us see the world as sacred and feel the inherent power we have within! Within our body, mind and spirit to commune with and enjoy the wealth inherent in life – effortlessly.

- The tantra wealth tools will help you increase your joy, creativity and overall richness.

- The beauty of effortlessness is you get to have what you desire and you get to enjoy the process along the way. The need for pushing, forcing and fear-based action falls away.

- The joy of effortlessness is in knowing the power you have and investing it with clarity and purpose knowing WUW is available for you always.

- The promise: that as you move forward through this program, you will find ease and flow. It is like you are going to be going to the School of Magic instead of the School of Hard Knocks that so many of us have been enrolled in.

Unquestioned Scarcity Agreements (Beliefs)

What follows is a list of 10 common unquestioned scarcity agreements that many of us hold. These are the ways we have come to agree that wealth in the world works and therefore must be true for us also. As you read through this list, notice which ones ping you – which ones feel you really believe and agree to.

1. *Scarcity Agreement #1* – That there is a <u>*separation*</u> between you and wealth and that wealth is outside of you, that you are separate from it

   o *Tantra teaches us* …that we are not separate or different, nor can we ever be separated from the prana, life force that is always prospering. This dualistic (separation) thinking is what tantra is teaching us to transcend.

2. *Scarcity Agreement #2* – That there is <u>*judgment*</u> around who gets to experience wealth. And that if we don't have money, time, energy, opportunity, luck, or education we will not be wealthy and prosperous.

   o *Tantra teaches us that when you perceive the prana of divinity within yourself – as yourself, you will eventually see it everywhere and you will see there is no judgement about prosperity – accept the judgements you make. (And this give us the freedom to choose anew).*

   A clear mind, free from prejudice, in touch with the sacred, sees grace pervading everything. – Tantra Shakti

3. *Scarcity Agreement #3* - That we are <u>unworthy</u> to have it and we are not sure we are worthy of prosperity or the good things we desire.

- *Tantra teaches us that the literal definition of Tantra is to "expand beyond all limitations. Including the misunderstanding that you are unworthy and anything less than divine."*

4. *Scarcity Agreement #4* – That prosperity is <u>*conditional*</u> and we have to do something correctly to experience wealth; success *is a result* of action.

   - *Tantra teaches us "we are all born with an equal capacity to achieve lasting fulfillment" Rod Stryker, The Four Desires*

5. *Scarcity Agreement #5* - That <u>*sacrifice*</u> is necessary and we must sacrifice something to have success, whether it is freedom, integrity, family, and health - something must be given up.

   - *Tantra teaches us "your thoughts energize whatever they focus on. This is true whether positive or negative. Since energy follows thought, attention must be collected and concentrated." Tantra Shakti*

6. *Scarcity Agreement #6* -That <u>*scarcity*</u> and limitation exist and there is a fixed-pie-of wealth; only so much money/love/resources/success to go around.

   - *Tantra teaches us "The challenge is to take into account the full measure of who you really are and use the positive force of your soul's desires…to lead you." Rod Stryker, The Four Desires.*

7. *Scarcity Agreement #7* – That prosperity and wealth require <u>*difficult*</u> effort and struggle.

   - *Tantra teaches us "your thoughts energize whatever they focus on." Tantra Shakti*

8. *Scarcity Agreement #8* – That success will <u>impact us negatively</u> so maybe we don't want success because it will change our lives and make people see us differently or treat us differently.

   - *Tantra teaches us "desire accompanied by discernment leads to spiritual growth/freedom." Tantra Shakti*

9. *Scarcity Agreement #9* - That our success dreams need to be *appropriate* or that we need to do something with a higher purpose or some other rules we agree to.

    o *Tantra teaches us "rather than judging desire, tantra recognizes desire as a constant and an expression of the soul's divinity. Growing the skills to apply tantra's exalted wisdom is expressly for achieving an exalted life."* Tantra Shakti SWEEEET! Right?

10. *Scarcity Agreement #10* - That an *outside force* can withhold our success from us. That it is up to some outside entity to decide or distribute success to us be it our boss or even "God".

    o *Tantra teaches us "self-knowledge and self-empowerment inspire you to become and to achieve things that reflect your Soul's glory. It is also the key that opens the door to freedom and success."* Tantra Shakti

The New Prosperity Agreements

Let these be your new prosperity agreements:

1. There is no <u>separation</u> between you and prosperity.

2. There are <u>no judgments</u> around the wealth you desire.

3. You are totally <u>worthy</u> to have wealth, in fact worthiness is not even a consideration.

4. Your wealth is <u>un-conditionally</u> yours and there is plenty for all.

5. Sacrifice is not necessary.

6. Scarcity and limitation <u>do not exist</u>.

7. Prosperity <u>flows</u>.

8. Prosperity energy will impact you as <u>you decide</u>.

9. Your wealth does not need to be <u>appropriate</u>.

10. Your prosperity can <u>never be withheld</u> from you.

Use the 8-Fold way to Choose Wealth

8-Fold Way is a tool for you to consciously direct your energy into whatever you are creating. Use the 8-fold way to direct prana in a focused and conscious way into the truth of your Prosperity & Wealth.

The 8-fold aspects of prospering prana focus are:

1. *Choosing*: Choose to focus your energy on your intention (sankulpa);

2. *Feeling*: Feel the excitement of your energy flowing into your desire;

3. *Speaking*: Speak with excitement about the fulfilment of your intention;

4. *Welcoming*: Welcome the fulfilment – open your heart to knowing it is done;

5. *Allowing*: Allow your desired intention to flow to you;

6. *Accepting*: Accept your desire, release any resistance you may have to it – soften to it.

7. *Noticing*: Notice the unfoldment in small and big ways;

8. *Enjoying*: Enjoy the entire journey, enjoy the flow, enjoy the prana, enjoy, enjoy, enjoy. Enjoyment is true appreciation.

———

The 8-Fold Way of Wealth:

1. CHOOSE IT – I choose to be unlimitedly wealthily

2. FEEL IT – I feel my unlimited connection to the ever-present, unlimited wealth energy – always flowing, unconditionally available to me

3. SPEAK IT – I speak (out loud) about my unlimited connection to wealth energy and how wonderful I feel as it surrounds me, in me, as me - effortlessly.

4. WELCOME IT – It feels so good to welcome my unlimited wealth. I marinate in the bounty, joy and unconditional flow, ever present.

5. ALLOW IT – I allow my unlimited connection to wealth – everyday. Every day, I spend time welcoming, allowing and enjoying all of the prosperity flowing to me.

6. ACCEPT IT – I accept I am unlimitedly wealthy (over and over until I agree).

7. NOTICE IT – I notice my unlimited connection to wealth and see how it shows up in every moment (from a bird song, to a cup of tea).

8. ENJOY – I enjoy my unlimited abundant connection to wealth – and I enjoy all the magic that flows from that. I so appreciate this feeling of unlimited, free-flowing grace and ease.

The link between Tantra and Prosperity

Tantra gives you direct experience of your richness. The practices help you directly experience your richness, the aliveness of your being and the prosperity that is flowing through you, to you, AS YOU – always and in all ways.

Journal Reflection

Date:

NUGGET I WANT TO REMEMBER

- How have you been investing your energy lately? What has gotten the majority of your time and attention? How do you feel most of the time?

- How would you define wealth right now?

- What if prana is wealth and wealth is prana? How does that change your perspective on wealth?

- Which of the Scarcity agreements impacted you? How?

- Does wealth have to mean hard work and difficult efforting? Why or Why not?

- What if you believed Wealth was not scarce, but like prana – everywhere present – how would that change your approach to day-to-day living?

Asana Practice: Journal Reflection   Date:

POST-PRACTICE
Journal about how you are feeling after the session practice. Be as detailed and specific as you can.

PHYSICALLY (note any changes and insights)

EMOTIONALLY

MENTALLY

OVERAL VITALITY (note any insights)

ONE WORD (how you feel):

PROSPERITY INSIGHTS
Journal about any insights you received in connection with your prosperity thinking and feeling

IMPORTANT NEW AWARENESSES AND IDEAS

NOTEWORTHY (message to yourself)

KEY NUGGET (an important understanding you will take from this)

ONE WORD (how you feel about prosperity now)

SESSION 2: CALM

CALM

CALM

All is well and you are safe

- In this session of the program, we create a safe, calm space so our minds can quiet and allow our bodies to relax. From this calm, tranquil mind and felt-sense...we feel stable. This felt-sense space of calm, safety and stability <u>becomes where we return to when our small-mind runs out of control into scarcity and worry.</u>

- This is a safe space and a calm place to explore and recognize your divinity. And to go into your inner temple, witness consciousness, and remember your true wealth and divine inheritance.

- Approach this time with excitement that what we are doing **is** bringing us closer to remembering and knowing our true prosperity, and the power of our Wealth-Source, our essential self!

Small-Scarcity-You and Big-Wealthy-You

- In Tantra, we learn to *know and feel* the difference between when Small-Ego-Mind (Small-Scarcity-You) is dominant and running the show or when we are in witness consciousness and our Big-Wealthy-Mind is remembering the truth of Who We Really Are – Divinity walking the earth.

- In this session, we will be investing in understanding when Small-Scary-You is dominant or when Big-Wealthy-You is active. As you become clear about this – you will have a powerful investment tool at your disposal – choice.

- Small-Scarcity-You feels cut-off and worried, limited and confined. Big-Wealth-You (Big-Mind) is the Supreme-Self and <u>knows</u> you are eternally connected to unlimited abundance and prosperity. You *are* unlimited abundance.

- Small Scarcity-You wonders about your innate value and worth. Big-Wealthy-You <u>remembers</u> how magnificent and divinely wealthy you truly are.

- Small-Scarcity-You falls prey to the insidious limitation messages of poverty and fix-pie ideas. Big-Wealthy-You <u>always is connected</u> to the wealth-stream-of-unlimited prosperity.

- Tantra teaches the ability to "discern" between the two and to be able to *feel and sense* the difference with "Witness Consciousness". So Big-Wealthy-You can help you choose to know, remember and feel connected.

You were meant to prosper

- You were not meant to suffer nor to be in want for anything (small-you thinks this.) You were meant to live in divine flow with the abundance of the planet. (Big-You, the Supreme-Self, knows this).

- It is divine will you prosper in every area of your life - to be a master in both the physical and spiritual realms. Know there is no separation between any realm.

- Big-Wealthy-You (your higher mind) is in constant communion with the universal cosmic resources in the unified field of divine love which is accessed through the heart chakra.

- According to yogic tradition, there will come a point where these opposites will have less impact and you will live in the Divine remembrance of your True-Self. (This is key to witness consciousness, knowing the difference between guidance from your soul and that from the thinking/ego mind.)

- You are developing the ability to choose WUW – Wealth-Unlimited-Wealth – and reside in the splendor of Big-Wealthy-You.

Other things Big-Wealthy-You knows

- Big-Wealthy-You knows that life on earth is meant to be **magical** – a **playground** - for you to focus and direct your energy into the desires of your heart. Little-Scarcity-You can think life is hard and not a playground and not all that magical. ☺ Elevate to your Big-Wealthy-Mind and let it remember and calm these old thoughts.

- Big-Wealthy-You feels and knows how lovingly this world is set up for you to be a **powerful creator**. Big-Wealthy-You (the supreme self) knows the law of attraction as an undeniable law, like the law of gravity, to be used for attracting your hearts desires. Little-Scarcity-You forgets how powerful you are. ☺ Elevate to your Big-Wealthy-Mind and let it remember and calm these old feelings.

- Big-Wealthy-You knows life on earth is set up a **fulfillment** machine…always saying YES to you. The energetic grid of the earth uses the law of attraction as an unbiased fulfillment mechanism for you to experience what you vibrate – unconditionally (no judgement) …the response if always – YES. Little-Scarcity-You forgets about the law of attraction and how it is constantly pulling what you focus on to you…and many times feels life is saying *NO, no way*. ☺ Elevate to your Big-Wealthy-Mind and let it remember and calm these old judgements.

- Big-Wealthy-You knows **well-being** is the essence of life. Well-being is woven into the fabric of life. The sun comes up, trees produce oxygen, so much love is facilitating life. Supreme-You knows this and basks in the ever-present wellbeing. Little-Scarcity-You worries constantly about your well-being. ☺ So, elevate to your Big-Wealthy-Mind and let it remember and calm these old approaches.

- Big-Wealthy-You knows life has all the **resources** you need in unlimited abundance and knows you have at your access everything needed to create what you desire. Little-Scarcity-You forgets and feels disconnected from the unlimited flow of resources. ☺ So, breathe! And elevate to your Big-Wealthy-Mind and let it remember and calm these old beliefs.☺

- Big-Wealthy-You knows that the nature of life is to **flow**, that life is always evolving and changing – this is exciting to Big-You. ☺

- Big-Wealthy-You knows that **Wealth IS** and that Wealth is experiencing itself AS you. Wealth is everywhere– because Prana is everywhere and flowing. Therefore, Wealth is always flowing, always prospering, always available. Big-Wealthy-You is experiencing its wealthy self here on earth in whatever wonderous ways you are inspired to. Scarcity-You wonders if it is good-enough, smart-enough, or practiced-enough? ☺ stop wondering…and know; elevate to your Big-Wealthy-Mind and let it remember and calm these old ideas.

Tantra approaches Calm through Moon Energy

- The moon practice comes at the beginning of our journey and works to calm the ego-mind. Stability in our mind helps us become still so we can sense and feel the difference between our Big-Mind and the Small-Ego mind that tends to dwell in scarcity and basically fear.

- It addresses the fact that your mind (like the moon) is always changing. The moon is feminine flow energy that makes it possible for us to integrate the increasing flow of abundance and prosperity into our lives.

- This practice gives us the capacity to remain centered and stable in the midst of change and at ease in the midst of transformation.

- The feminine side of the body is often referred to the **left** side of the body and connects us to our nurturing, intuitive and emotional side and regardless of gender, we all have both feminine and masculine energy. The **feminine side is considered** cooling, calming, Yin, **moon energy**.

- Cultivating calm in the asana practice: focus on forward bends and/or twists with fewer poses and longer holds with the intention to become still in the pose (less tweaking and adjusting).

- Cultivate Calm in pranayama/breath practice: use 1:2 breathing (where exhale is twice as long as inhale). For example, breathe in for 4 counts and breathe out for 8 counts.

- Cultivate Stability in pranayama/breath practice: use 1:1 breathing (where exhale is same length as inhale).

- Meditation: "I am not my thoughts – I AM that which is watching my mind think". I AM the unlimited presence, life force, that perceives all.

Develop the wiliness to receive

- Receiving is us naturally learning to lower our resistance and receive the wealth of life to flow to us and through us.

- Scarcity-Ego-Mind tends to resist as it is trying to protect us from life. Small-Scarcity-You has developed safety approaches that end up acting like blockages and resistance to the flow of prana.

- Notice the breath. We breathe in, we receive, we breathe out, we share and give of ourselves. Each moment, we are in this wonderful effortless giving and receiving dance with life.

- But many of us have a hard time with the idea of receiving and allowing ourselves the pleasure of experiencing free and clear. Many things given are not always given free and clear. But when we are talking about Prana-Wealth-Energy it is always available free and clear - with no strings attached. Big-Wealthy-You knows this and can calm the fears of Scarcity-You

- There are many other felt-sense ideas for receiving. Play with feeling these: allow, welcome, enjoy, release, relax, flow, accept, recognize, remember, greet, embrace, appreciate, relish, love, bask...You get it - invest in releasing resistance to receiving by cultivating these energies instead.

- Tantra teaches us how to release resistances that are the focus of Small-Scarcity-Mind and allow us to flow and be in flow with the prana of life.

A reading from the Ashtavakra Gita

With the pincers of truth

I have plucked from the dark corners of my heart

the thorn of many judgements

♥ and I sit inside my own splendor

Work or pleasure, duty or discrimination

duality or non-duality - what do they mean to me?

what is yesterday or tomorrow or today?

what is space or eternity?

♥ I sit inside my own radiance

What is the self or the not self

what is thinking or not thinking what is good or not good

♥ I sit inside my own splendor

♥ I sit in my own radiance and I have no fear

This is my true voice of the self

Waking dreaming sleeping what are they to me – or even ecstasy

 what is far or near - outside or inside - gross or subtle

♥ I sit inside my own splendor

Delving the mind or the highest meditation – all the world and all its works

Life or death what are they to me?

♥ I sit inside my own radiance

Why talk of wisdom or even oneness – why talk of these?

Now I live inside my heart –

♥ I live inside my own splendor – Lord Shiva

- When we have accepted the identity of personhood – the mind (Small-You) will tell you - work more, study more, look harder, try more, you are almost there – well maybe you will never get there – someday – but not today.

- Big-Wealth-You – sits inside your own splendor. Knowing, there is nothing to fix or to change. You are already - you are already the Self. But for a long time dreaming you are separate from the Supreme-Self

- Now rest inside your own splendor. Sit in silence with witness consciousness (Big-Mind) and marinate in your own radiance - your own silence - your own prosperity and peace. Knowing there is neither end nor beginning for you. There is nothing, nothing, nothing, apart from the Supreme Self.

- There is nothing apart from the Supreme Self.
  Everything is the Supreme Self.
  Know this and be happy.

Journal Reflection   Date:

NUGGET I WANT TO REMEMBER

- Do I know how to create a safe, calm space for myself? If I did, I would…

- What if I am not my thoughts? What if I AM that which is watching my mind think? What if I AM the unlimited presence, life force, that perceives all? How does that change my day?

- What things would Big-Wealthy you do that scarcity you is keeping you from?

- How do I feel about receiving? Am I good at it? Why or why not?

Asana Practice: Journal Reflection   Date:

POST-PRACTICE
Journal about how you are feeling after the session practice. Be as detailed and specific as you can.

PHYSICALLY (note any changes and insights)

EMOTIONALLY

MENTALLY

OVERAL VITALITY (note any insights)

ONE WORD (how you feel):

PROSPERITY INSIGHTS

Journal about any insights you received in connection with your prosperity thinking and feeling

IMPORTANT NEW AWARENESSES AND IDEAS

NOTEWORTHY (message to yourself)

KEY NUGGET (an important understanding you will take from this)

ONE WORD (how you feel about prosperity now)

SESSION 3: AWAKEN

AWAKEN

AWAKEN

Awaken to That Which You Really Are

- The third stage of the Tantra of Prosperity is the Sun (Surya) stage – where we awaken to that which you really are: divine energy (prana shatki) taking on human form for a bit. The focus in this stage is around prana (life force as it accumulates in the solar plexus and heart center) and your relationship to it. There are 2 primary intentions: first to awaken to the awareness of who/what you really are and second, to expand your ability to hold more of your life force and radiate it fully.

- In our last session we experienced our stability through the moon energy, it is from that stability that the sun can shine fully and you can hold the abundance that you came from and still are.

- As you awaken to that which you really are – you will realize you do not have to earn it – you are it! You do not have to earn prosperity – you are it, you do not have to earn wealth – You are it. Small-Scarcity-You forgets this – Big-Wealthy-You never forgets this. Like the sun, we **radiate** all the time, even when we don't see it or feel like it.

Appreciate Who You Really Are

- Developing a deep understanding and appreciation of Who You Really Are and what you bring to the table is a vital step in your wealth consciousness journey. Allow yourself to see your radiance, feel your radiance and experience your radiance in every way – everyday. That is what we are up to.

- This is a critical point in the process because if you are not awake to Who You Really Are you will not feel empowered or valuable enough to tap into the Wealth that is available to you. Through this practice and session, we are tapping into our natural empowerment, capability and strength. We are ready, willing and able.

- Self-awareness and self-appreciation enable us to live fully and joyfully steeped in the truth of our self-worth. And in many ways our self-worth impacts our net-worth. Because people who have a sense of their innate worth make different kinds of decisions and take actions that honor their value.

- Awakening is wondrous because knowing you are a glorious, divine, amazing light being changes how you walk and live. Who You Really Are is a light-being having a human experience—instead of a human having a once-in-a-while-divine experience.

- Many of us feel insignificant and this dims our internal light. As we journey forth developing our wealth consciousness, we learn Who We Really Are and our power to create. We become beacons of light – way showers of how glorious it can be to live on this magical place called earth…and Big-Wealthy-You enjoys this greatly.

Awaken to Your Uniqueness

- As you Awaken to Who You Really Are and flow with the natural things you are interested in, you are investing in your magic – and it will affect the world around you. As you honor yourself by listening to the urges of your heart, you will feel drawn to certain things that resonate with you. And if you allow yourself to follow these urges and invest in them with your life energy, you craft a very unique & wealth-filled life... one that is uniquely fulfilling to you in so many ways.

- You matter and you are important *as you are*. Your unique desires and approaches to how you live your life enhance the whole of humanity. You never know *how you being your uniqueness* will impact another person.

- Honor your uniqueness. Listen to your unique body. Respect your unique urges and feelings; this is you in flow with life flowing uniquely through you. Big-Wealthy-You is comfortable and confident with this.

"As we let our light shine,
we unconsciously give other people permission to do the same.
As we are liberated from our own fear, our presence actually liberates others."
– Marianne Williamson

Awaken To You as Worthy

- Your value is not because of what you do, who you know or how you are educated or any of the other conditional messages about value. You are valuable and valued just because of Who You Really Are.

- Most of us are very hard on ourselves, feeling we are not worthy of the good things of life or that we are inadequate. Inadequacy, inferiority, and the similar not-enoughness beliefs we hold about ourselves keep us bound to limitation and from the wealth we wish to experience. It is time to acknowledge and appreciate Who You Really Are so these old feelings can start to fade and new possibilities allowed to flow.

- To know you are worthy of good things is at the core of wealth consciousness. Big-Wealthy-You knows your sense of value and feels empowered, strong and very rich.

Awaken to you as Powerful Creator

- Awakening to our creative power means we to see ourselves as energy masters that mold the clay of life into whatever shapes and experience we desire. It is divine play.

- Those of us that forget our power to create, end up feeling like a victim of life. And the energies of helpless, hopeless, depression etc. are the direct result of forgetting our creating power.

- The joy of conscious creating, via energy investing, gives you the ability and excitement to realize your power. As we embrace our creative power, we become a beacon of light and a force for change. We stand at the helm of our ship and use our internal tools of conscious creation to mold the life we choose and Big-Wealthy-You enjoys this greatly.

Awaken to you as Infinitely Respected

- You are honored greatly, known as powerful and capable. You are the master creator of your life. Your life is your opportunity to create and choose whatever you want – however you want...no judgment.

- This is your endowment as the spark of God that came to earth to experience 3D.

- No-one or no-thing is deciding if you get to experience that which you say you are creating. Learn the tools of energy that tantra teaches and you have the energy skills to create.

- If you need help or support it flows without judgment. If you ask for something, you must want it or need it for your life creation. And because you are infinitely respected as the master creator of your life, the answer is always – yes, ok, as you wish! Big-Wealth-You knows this and plays with energy like a master potter forming a lump of clay into a glorious bowl.

Awaken to Your Body As Amazing

- Your body is a divine transmitter/receiver. The chakra system makes conscious creating possible. The serpent energy at the base of the spine can be coaxed up through the spine (sushumna) to the pineal gland in the brain (third-eye). Moving this energy is how we radiate and create.

- Each chakra has intelligence – mini-brains, that support our full experience of our divinity on the earth.

- Your breath is the mechanism that actives this system.

- Your body is designed to easily and effortlessly communicate and commune with Unlimited-Source – and tantra shows the way.

Awaken To You as Sri Prana Shatki Energy Radiating

- Sri is resplendent, grace, wealth, prosperity, beauty, luster. Prana Shakti is the primordial cosmic energy that governs all physical functions. Awaken to yourself as sri prana shatki...resplendent, divine-energy personified.

"Our deepest fear is not that we are inadequate. Our deepest fear is that we are powerful beyond measure. It is our Light, not our Darkness, that most frightens us." – Marianne Williamson

Tantra approaches Awakening through Sun Energy

- The sun stage is where you focus on deepening your connection to the life force – to awaken you to a world that is normally unseen. You become capable of seeing and feeling the unseen wealth force that is life.

- The more energy you can contain and build, the more you can use it to propel yourself out of your intrinsic "small-body-mind-scarcity" – and connect to the infinite Big-Wealth-Spring.

- As tantra yoga is the science of energy management, the sun practice fuels your journey.

- The breathing technique called *Prana Dharana* is the root of the tantric practices…as it focuses on awakening and expanding the third-eye – your connection to cosmic consciousness. So, the practice of Prana Dharana becomes the conduit that makes it possible to thrive in any and all aspects of life.

- *Prana Dharana Practice:* Building our sensitivity to and awareness of Prana around the third-eye center.

The practice to cultivate the sun

- Asana: the physical practice focuses on backbends and lateral movement; poses that expand and enliven.

- Breath: Emphasizes developing inhalation – with pauses after inhale during the asana practice and in pranayama.

- Pranayama: *Prana Dharana*

- Bandha (lock): Building vital life force. Focus on the chin lock or *jalandhara bandha* to build the life force in and around the heart and core. *Uddyana Bandha* to create energy and light around the solar plexus. *Mula Bandha* internalizes mind and energy around the base of the spine.

- Meditation: Primary focusing is to deepen your relationship to light and RADIATE - spread it out into the world.

- Bhavana (felt-sense): Cultivate your connection to the life-force that animates all of life – and to build upon the awareness that your body is a vessel of energy.

- As you do this – do not get caught in duality thinking, your body is a vessel AND it is energy.

Radiate as the Sun that You Are

- Radiate as the glorious presence that you are. It is from this place that you are comfortable to take risks. It is not having everything perfectly laid out and it allows you to experience creativity in a way that when you're managing to make sure you are safe you many times can't do.

- Release the doubts that you mind might throw in...CALM yourself to remember to the Awakened awareness of your power, and radiance.

Remember this poem from Marianne Williamson:

Our deepest fear is not that we are inadequate.
Our deepest fear is that we are powerful beyond measure.

It is our light, not our darkness that most frightens us.
We ask ourselves, who am I to be brilliant, gorgeous, talented fabulous?
Actually, who are you not to be? You are a child of god.

Your playing small does not serve the world.

There is nothing enlightened about shrinking so that other people won't feel insecure around you.
We are all meant to shine, as children do.
We were born to make manifest the glory of God that is within us.

It's not just in some of us; it's in everyone!

And as we let our own light shine, we unconsciously give other people permission to do the same.

As we are liberated from our own fear, our presence automatically liberates others!

RADIATE YOUR LIGHT!

OUR DEEPEST FEAR IS NOT THAT **WE ARE INADEQUATE.** OUR DEEPEST FEAR IS THAT WE ARE **POWERFUL BEYOND MEASURE. IT IS OUR LIGHT,** NOT OUR DARKNESS THAT MOST FRIGHTENS US. WE ASK OURSELVES, WHO AM I TO BE

BRILLIANT, GORGEOUS, TALENTED, FABULOUS? ACTUALLY, WHO ARE YOU NOT TO BE? YOU ARE A CHILD OF GOD. YOUR PLAYING SMALL DOES NOT SERVE **THE WORLD.**

THERE IS NOTHING ENLIGHTENED ABOUT SHRINKING SO THAT OTHER PEOPLE WON'T FEEL INSECURE AROUND YOU. **WE ARE ALL MEANT TO SHINE, AS CHILDREN DO. WE WERE BORN** TO MAKE MANIFEST THE GLORY OF GOD THAT IS WITHIN US. **IT'S NOT JUST IN SOME OF US; IT'S IN EVERYONE.** AND AS WE LET OUR OWN LIGHT SHINE, WE UNCONSCIOUSLY GIVE OTHER PEOPLE **PERMISSION TO DO THE SAME. AS WE ARE** LIBERATED FROM OUR OWN FEAR, OUR PRESENCE AUTOMATICALLY **LIBERATES OTHERS.**

— MARIANNE WILLIAMSON —

Journal Reflection	Date:

NUGGET I WANT TO REMEMBER

- Do you want to awaken to who/what you really are? If yes? Why would you say? If not – why do you think? What does awaken to who you really are mean to you?

- What are you naturally got at (your gifts). Do you consider these part of your prosperity?

- Do you feel worthy? Elaborate...

- Do you feel powerful? Elaborate…

- Do you feel you create? Or could create if…

- Please re-read the Marianne Williamson quote – and think of yourself as you read it – what things go through your mind? Honestly…

Asana Practice: Journal Reflection   Date:

POST-PRACTICE
Journal about how you are feeling after the session practice. Be as detailed and specific as you can.

PHYSICALLY (note any changes and insights)

EMOTIONALLY

MENTALLY

OVERAL VITALITY (note any insights)

ONE WORD (how you feel):

PROSPERITY INSIGHTS

Journal about any insights you received in connection with your prosperity thinking and feeling

IMPORTANT NEW AWARENESSES AND IDEAS

NOTEWORTHY (message to yourself)

KEY NUGGET (an important understanding you will take from this)

ONE WORD (how you feel about prosperity now)

SESSION 4:
ALCHEMIZE

ALCHEMIZE

ALCHEMIZE

Intentionally Transforming Energy

- Alchemizing is a powerful process of transforming our old scarcity energy agreements and feelings, which are not serving us any longer, and making the energy available for something greater and aligned with our new wealth investment intentions.

- In this section, we will learn the process of alchemizing and use it to transform the energy of our old scarcity agreements

Learn to release & transform

- Traditionally, alchemizing is the process of turning lead into gold. It is a transmutation and transformation process where you take a base metal and change it into a precious metal using **fire** and heat (which we will do in our asana practice).

- As we let go and release the old beliefs, we transform the energy that those beliefs and behaviors occupied to make it available for new experiences that are flourishing, enlivening and prospering.

- If you stop for a moment and feel into old energy beliefs, they probably feel heavy, confining, draining or limiting. These negative feelings and many others like worry, anger, frustration, blame, shame and not-enoughness – are all a form of *resistance*.

- Resistance feels like a blockage to the natural abundant Wealth flow that is at the core our of life. Release the resistance and we become available to be in flow and to feel the Wealth of life flow through us.

- Alchemize makes you available for the magic of life. And there is so much magic, so much magic. Through this process, we are making ourselves available and able to accept and enjoy the magic!

The Tantra Fire Practice

- The fire practice we will be doing works with agni (fire) for unleashing sprit.

- You will work with inhale and exhale retention in the asana to create a powerful internal focus (and flame).

- Maha mudra will be used to dissolve stagnation in the lower 3 chakras, as it is a spinal extension which creates space in the lower back.

- All 3 bandhas will be used to contain and build the energy in the within the core of your body. Jalandhara bandha, (at the throat) and mula bandha at the perineum and uddiyana bandha at the navel center.

- Throughout the practice, return to the sense of calm (moon) so you remain stable while the transformation happens. Thus, being the witness to the process.

- Finally, as the fire builds you will use some for the transformation and keep some for assimilation and creation.

The Alchemizing Process has 5 Steps:

- **Step 1. Acknowledge It** - See the scarcity agreement/energy pattern and its associated feeling(s). Acknowledge how it *makes you feel* - because we cannot change that which we stay unconscious to. See it as it is - without judgment.

- **Step 2. Accept It** – Accept the truth of how you *really* feel. This means to not fight against what is showing up right now. Be present. Don't pretend that your feelings are not at play. See if you feel angry, or if you feel overwhelmed or hopeless? Allow yourself to get clarity and accept that is how you really feel.

- **Step 3. Release It** – symbolically and tangibly. Release is basically surrendering the agreement and its associated feelings. Surrender is not weak or wimpy. It is a way to stop the fight and quell the resistance. As we stop fighting how we really feel, we honor ourselves and our experience – and as we breathe, we start the process of transformation – our breath transforms the energy.

- **Step 4. Thank It** - and become peaceful with it. At this point, feel thankful to the old agreement for what it has given you and taught you. Feel thankful for it giving you the gift of insight. As you thank it for helping you, protecting you and giving you what you needed *at the time,* you are alchemizing it from something that was a problem to a friend with a gift.

- **Step 5. Replace It** - Reach for a new wealth agreement that feels better. You are now going to make a powerful investment in a new idea and a felt-sense of a fresh wealth experience and perspective.

Journal Step 1 – Acknowledge It: See the scarcity agreement and its associated feeling(s)

Start journaling about a worry or reoccurring idea you have been carrying around and noticing takes up a lot of your energy. Journal about what does not feel good. Just start letting a stream of consciousness flow, writing with the intent to get clarity on the issue and the feelings inside of it – "unpack it" so to speak. Throughout this journaling time, just write. Notice and acknowledge. Don't censor or worry about being politically correct – the more honest you are about how you really feel, the better the clarity you will get.

Ask yourself:

- What is the scarcity notion I keep holding onto? What seems to be at the root of it?

Journal Step 2 – Accept the truth of how you really feel

Ask yourself:

- If I were honest, and it was ok to feel how I feel – I would say I feel _____? Journal your truth.
- What is the message inside of the feeling? Are there any flashes of memories or thoughts that arise as you go deeper into the feeling? Just notice.

Invoke the Violet Flame

- The violet flame is a powerful transmutation energy that raises the energies of lower density to higher vibration, e.g. from scarcity to prosperity. It is a powerful vibration that burns through resistance and blockage.

- Invoking the Violet Flame as you proceed with your alchemizing process will provide the quickest path to liberation. It supports the transmutation of trying circumstances, suffering, problems and anxieties...it is a powerful alchemy tool.

- Invocation to violet flame[1]

  > I call upon the Elohim of the Violet Ray,
  > To pour Divine Transmutation through all that I AM.
  >
  > I call upon the Amethyst Ray, to transform every cell,
  > every atom of my bodies into Higher light.
  >
  > I call upon the Violet Flame to burn within my soul,
  > and release all veils that separate me from spirit.
  >
  > I call upon the violet flame to burn away my illusions,
  > to burn away my resistances, and transmute my fear to love.

The Power of Surrender

- At this point, there is clarity. Now, a choice is to be made. Are you ready to release? Are you ready to surrender this old energy? Are you ready to let it go and let it be transmuted?

- If you are ready, use your breath, the violet flame and the fire asana practice to alchemize the energy. Allow how you feel to arise and breathe through it. If you are worried allow the worry to come and breathe into it and feel it move through you. If you are scared be scared, breathe deeply, you might find it fades or disappears. If you are disappointed be disappointed.

---

[1] Page 118 of book: *What is Lightbody*, by Archangel Ariel Channeled by Tashira Rachi-ren.

- Surrender the fight. Let the fire of the violet flame transmute the energies. Note: Surrendering is not defeat. Surrender is to release resistance and stop the struggle.

- Feel the relief that surrender brings which allows the freshness of life to flow – unimpeded.

- Surrendering your old approaches allows for unexpected possibilities and unplanned resolutions to be seen - at some point.

- As you do this, you will feel the energy arise and your mind will want to jump in and fix it or justify it. <u>Don't</u>. Just let the feeling be there and feel it – and breathe. Also notice any other associated feelings that are in there to be "unpacked". After you feel fear, you might then feel anger, then you might feel rage or exhaustion. Let it come, let it be, let it come to the surface freely. As it arises let the energy of the emotion flow (tears, anger, yelling – it's all ok). This is the energy releasing...there is nothing more you need to do really – but notice it, let it flow and let it go.

- Breathe and feel the tension release from your shoulders, neck and torso. Breathe deeply and relax. Give yourself permission to release the tension, release the anger, release the frustration. Feel lighter and lighter.

Journal Step 3 – Release & Surrender

Ask yourself:

- Is there anything I noticed as I allowed the release? How did my body feel? How did my head feel? What insights or ideas came to me?

Journal Step 4 – Thank it and become peaceful with it.

This step is quite beautiful in that we can now see how the scarcity energy was part of our journey which brought us here. Somehow this old scarcity agreement served us and we experienced it for a reason. So, Thank you. It may have helped us survive and get through life to this point...so thank you.

You might even want to bless it. Give it your best energy and your highest thoughts. Feel it was a friend come to help you move in a new direction.

For the most part, after we become peaceful and thankful for an issue it is mostly transformed – the energy is transformed from frustration to clarity, from anger to understanding and this takes the disempowerment out of the equation.

Ask yourself:
- What has this old agreement given me and taught me? What have I learned about how I feel and how I have been living my life as a result of this old scarcity belief?
- What new insights, understanding or clarity do I have now that I want to bring forward?

Journal Step 5 - Reach for a new wealth agreement that feels better.

Now is the time to reach for a new thought or feeling when it comes to your wealth. Reaching for something greater, make a new investment that feels good to you. You are now going to make a powerful investment in a new idea and a felt-sense of a fresh wealth experience and perspective. Because one of the most effective tools for dealing with an old experience is to give it a different meaning. We take on a different attitude about the past hurt and we acknowledge the hidden gift in it.

Ask yourself:
- If I were to reach for a new wealth agreement that feels better, what would it be? What would I start investing in instead of the old limitation?
- What would I rather feel than the anger, frustration and whatever I mentioned in Step 2? *Maybe draw a picture or find a picture or find a quote that embodies the new agreement and felt-sense you are choosing instead...*

The Power of Alchemy

- Now that you understand the power of alchemy – which is energy transmutation from one state to another. From

- We create through the process of alchemy - transmuting our life energy from one state to anther – like cars, houses, relationships, money.

- Energy is neither created or destroyed – it just takes on different forms. We alchemize money into our home improvement, we alchemize our life energy into that which we desire.

- The next 4 sessions of this program will show you how to do that.

A quote from Mary Oliver poem – The Journey

One day you finally knew
what you had to do, and began,
Though the voices around you kept shouting
their bad advice –
Though the whole house
Began to tremble
You felt the old tug at your ankles
"Mend my life" - each voice cried.
But you didn't stop
You knew what you had to do.

Journal Reflection   Date:

NUGGET I WANT TO REMEMBER

- How do you feel after doing this process?

- Is there anything that came up that you want to remember or acknowledge?

- How do you feel about the idea of surrender? What would be a word you would use?

Asana Practice: Journal Reflection   Date:

POST-PRACTICE
Journal about how you are feeling after the session practice. Be as detailed and specific as you can.

PHYSICALLY (note any changes and insights)

EMOTIONALLY

MENTALLY

OVERAL VITALITY (note any insights)

ONE WORD (how you feel):

PROSPERITY INSIGHTS

Journal about any insights you received in connection with your prosperity thinking and feeling

IMPORTANT NEW AWARENESSES AND IDEAS

NOTEWORTHY (message to yourself)

KEY NUGGET (an important understanding you will take from this)

ONE WORD (how you feel about prosperity now)

SESSION 5: ALIGN

ALIGN

ALIGN

Align to the Unlimited Wealth Energy

- A key skill we are developing is our ability to *align* and *stay aligned* to the never-ending flow of Prosperity, Love and Joy that is around us always and in all ways. Alignment is a choice and a practice.

- Alignment allows you create at your highest potential and easily allows you to receive a wealth of unexpected opportunities that you could not orchestrate alone through effort.

- As a part of this experience, you are finding *your* unique felt-sense (or energy vibration) of alignment to the Ever-Present and unlimited-wealth, abundance and prosperity.

- With the tools of tantra, you are learning how to cultivate the energy vibrations (focus) within yourself - at will. It takes a bit of practice – investment – and once you get the hang of it, you will find that you are making choices that ultimately align you to the life experience you desire. **This ability to choose how you feel and focus your vibration into alignment is your ticket to prosperity.**

Remember – the golden rule of prana: energy follows thought – (what you put your attention on expands)

- Your chakra system is your energy vibration system – that supports your alignment and connection to the Divine. Aligning these centers in love – allows prana to flow.

- Your Heart – the doorway to the divine - love puts us in the center of our splendor.

- Also, part of this Alignment session, we get clear about what makes us feel *aligned* (e.g. joyful, fulfilled, prosperous and generally wonderful). We will also spend time understanding what takes us *out of alignment* and throws us into the felt-sense of fear, worry, doubt and general anxiety/scarcity (out-of-alignment).

The Chakras: The Energy System of Your Body

- The chakras are part of your subtle energy anatomy, just as your spine is part of your physical anatomy. And they provide the conduit for conscious creation. And you can focus your energetic power that is inherent in your chakra system to intentionally align to unlimited wealth.

- Aligning your energy to flow through your energy anatomy is one of the great powers and benefits of tantra yoga.

- Your body is amazing and has the **built-in capability** to move direct and focus energy to facilitate a life of great joy! *you were designed to be a powerful energy transmitter that is meant to align to and have access to all of grace abundance and magic of divinity!*

Adhikara: The transformation of Matter *to* Energy *to* Full Divine Consciousness – aligning matter to the divine

- Adhikara denotes the process by which you and your practice evolve to shift from matter focus *to* energy focus *to* unlimited consciousness.

  - o Matter focus is an orientation where we are primarily focused on the body (day-to-day doing) – and can feel small and limited.

  - o Energy focus is an orientation to feeling the vibration in all matter – and we start to realize we are so much more – we are prana.

  - o Consciousness is where our limited perception dissolves into oneness with all-of-reality – divinity is all there is.

- Alignment is the process of consciously moving from a matter orientation (I am only my body-limited) to an energy orientation (I am prana) and ultimately alignment (unity) with All-That-Is (I AM Unlimited).

The Energy Arrow of Alignment

- Your inner alignment is like an arrow of great force and focused energy and when it is combined with an elevated heart-felt emotion like love, abundance and prosperity – great things happen.

- Alignment guides you to <u>positively</u>, with a radiant heart, <u>focus</u> your emotions, thoughts and actions into a single arrow of unified belief directed at the target of your highest possible success.

- The simple consistent act of choosing to live in alignment with your Divine-Essence's daily guidance, accelerates positive manifestations in your life with extraordinary momentum.

- Alignment connects you to the Ever-Present-Prana-intelligence that makes for divine synchronicity – so you can experience the satisfying perfection of your alignment.

- Let go of resistance and be swept into momentous flow of positive energy taking you where you soul authentically wants to go.

- Aligning your thoughts emotions and actions shoots your awareness like an arrow into the joyful power of unlimited abundance and satisfaction.

Invest in Understanding What Puts You IN Alignment with feeling good and wealthy.

- The feeling of alignment is as different for each of us, as the things that bring us into the feeling-state of Alignment like ease, grace and satisfaction – basically residing in your heart center.

- Get clarity on what *you* have noticed puts you into the state of feeling that "all is well", that life is good; that feeling of peace or contentment.

  - **Appreciating – noticing what works, enjoying, basking, thanking…all very aligned and in your heart.**
  - **Meditation** - the process of quieting the mind, slowing down, helps us feel at peace, relaxed and refreshed.
  - Being with their **family, friends** or **children** allows them to relax to the point they feel at peace and have moments of alignment.

o The act of **creating** something is one of the best ways to experience align-ment.

o Doing something you **love,** being in nature, gardening, playing with your pet, doing yoga, working out or being physical.

Ask yourself:

- What the things in my life make me feel aligned to grace, ease and satisfaction? What are the things, people, experiences, or moments that give me a sense of non-resistance and open-heartedness? What just feels good to me and makes me feel aligned to and with abundance and love?

Invest in Understanding What Takes You OUT of Alignment with feeling good and wealthy.

- When we are out of alignment, our energy feels blocked. We feel insecure, unclear, worried, resistant, small, heavy, doubtful, disempowered, weakened, conditional, and frustrated. Above all, we feel limited and scarce. Here is a short list of ideas of things that can take you out of alignment:

  - **Trying to get the "right answer"** or do the right thing or be right. Finding the right answer can lead to a win/lose (scarcity) mindset.
  - **Feeling like we are not good enough,** have not done enough, am not enough. Inadequacy and not-enoughness in any form is non-aligned
  - **Arguing, fighting,** talking politics, or anything where you are on opposing sides usually takes us out of alignment.
  - **Poor health** or health issues make us not feel good. And not feeling good is the opposite of alignment.
  - **Money.** Actually, it is *worry* about money and all the corresponding thoughts, feelings and emotions that feel crappy and not aligned.
  - **Guilt**, feeling bad about anything. Guilt eats up tons of energy, leaves us feeling low, heavy, depleted and poor; which is the opposite of aligned.
  - **Being hard on yourself.** Nothing takes you out of alignment faster than being hard on yourself and trying to fix yourself.
  - Other things that *can* throw you out of alignment (in no particular order): traffic jams, news shows, some talk radio, waiting in line, your email not working, not having milk, running out of coffee, too many people in yoga class, not getting the gift you wanted, running out of gas, haters, losing at Wii, clutter, fashion magazines, seeing/hearing of someone who has lost weight and makes you feel guilty, politics, judging, comparing, assessing, dehydration, demands, over-scheduling, no food in the refrigerator, aggressive music, Facebook, Instagram where everyone looks like they are living way better than you, violent movies, make-you-feel-inadequate commercials, too many commercials.

  - Key point: there are little things everyday things that can throw you out of alignment because you feel frustration, anger, worry, etc. *It is the feelings that result from the above things that are important.* Because the resulting feelings are misaligned causing resistance to the prosperous energy around you.

Ask yourself:

- What the things in my life take me out of alignment with the flow of wealth energy? What are the things, people, experiences, past experiences, thoughts, or moments that exhaust me? Frustrate me? Make me feel guilty? Worried? Poor? Resentful?

Aligning is choosing to sit inside your own splendor

- Choose your Focus. Focus on the things that put you in alignment instead of the things that do not. As we walk on the earth, we can see things that seemly disturb us, but this is not to be focused upon – remember the golden rule of prana – energy follows thought.

- The thought of love and the highest splendor is what we focus on... **I sit inside my own splendor!** Not, I *hope* to sit inside my own splendor – I SIT inside my own splendor.

I sit inside my own splendor – let that be how you walk in your day today. Remind yourself of it and say, I sit inside my own radiance – I am inside my own splendor.

I am aligned with love – in love – as love.

NUGGET I WANT TO REMEMBER

- Do you think alignment is a choice? Do you think you can practice alignment?

- Where you surprised by what alignment is and what takes you in and out of alignment?

- How much time, energy and attention do you end up investing in out-of-alignment things? Is there anyway you can be in alignment while doing them?

Asana Practice: Journal Reflection   Date:

POST-PRACTICE
Journal about how you are feeling after the session practice. Be as detailed and specific as you can.

PHYSICALLY (note any changes and insights)

EMOTIONALLY

MENTALLY

OVERAL VITALITY (note any insights)

ONE WORD (how you feel):

PROSPERITY INSIGHTS

Journal about any insights you received in connection with your prosperity thinking and feeling

IMPORTANT NEW AWARENESSES AND IDEAS

NOTEWORTHY (message to yourself)

KEY NUGGET (an important understanding you will take from this)

ONE WORD (how you feel about prosperity now)

SESSION 6: ATTRACT

ATTRACT

ATTRACT

Attracting energy is magnetizing energy.

- Choose to focus on what you want, align to it, vibrate AS it.

- What you put your attention, energy and focus on is you attract. (note: if we focus on what we don't want we are attracting that to us also).

- In this attracting section, we will understand how to magnetize or activate experiences we want – by intentionally cultivating a felt sense of wealth and prosperity - now.

Attracting Basics:

1. Start from a good feeling - ALIGNED - place –feel aligned to unlimited love and wealth. this is why yoga or meditation in the morning sets your day up for flow.)

   - Tantra helps you align to and remember you are part of, and are a unique expression of Unlimited-Prosperity-Energy.

2. Clarify what you want – what you want to FEEL like.

3. It is ok to be general about the wealth and prosperity you are desiring. In fact – be general – as in I AM wealthy...with no specifics – this allows life to surprise and delight you.

4. Vibrate AS wealth & prosperity. Be the change you seek – meaning – walk through your days feeling and vibrating wealth, **speaking** prosperously, **thinking** abundantly to attract wealth.

5. Release resistance and "wondering IF". Doubt extinguishes the fire of desire.

6. Feelize Wealth & Prosperity - seeing your desire in your mind as well as feeling it and getting excited about it in your body

7. Know it is done.

Start from a good feeling – Aligned place

- The tools of tantra (asana, pranayama, meditation) teach us how to ALIGN our energy into an empowered place.

- Remember that you are part of and an expression of a timeless Being-Energy.

- Begin to breathe, first into the belly (diaphragmatic breathing), this brings the mind into the body and into the Present moment. Move into full spinal breath, feeling the spine grow longer on inhale and stabilize on exhale, navel to spine.

- Move into your Heart – put your attention on your heart center.

- Asana: dynamic movement that keeps you connected to this breath. Movement on the breath. At this point, the breath is more important than the asana. Chanting on exhale will also build the connection to breath. Spend time in Savasana to integrate breath and body/mind.

- Pranayama: Focus on building Prana or Presence in the Third Eye Center. See Light as a Living Presence.

- Meditate on this Presence as a Living Presence imbuing you with Energy and Light –a state of bliss and peace.

Clarify what you want

- How does it FEEL to HAVE wealth and prosperity? Create the FEELING sense of what you are desiring.

- You might want to start with what you don't want and flip it to what you do – and that is why it ok to be general.

- It is ok to be general about the wealth and prosperity you are desiring. In fact – be general – as in I AM wealthy...with no specifics – this allows life to surprise and delight you.

Vibrate AS wealth & prosperity.

- Gandhi said: Be the change you seek – meaning – walk through your days feeling and vibrating wealth, **speaking** prosperously, **thinking** abundantly to attract wealth.

- Do not meditate "on" the desire – meditate "AS" the desire fulfilled.

Release resistance of doubt, worry...etc.

- "Wondering if" is not an aligned use of your energy.

- Doubt extinguishes the fire of desire.

Feelize Wealth & Prosperity

- Feelizing is visualizing and feeling together - seeing our desire in our mind as well as feeling it and getting excited about it in our body (like jumping for joy) as we see it happen in our life.

- Engage your creative mind when we visualize and see our vision happening. We engage our body when we emote and feel our desire.

- NOW - Focus on it happening NOW – not someday, feel it happening now.

Know it is done.

- When you have a desire, the mechanics for its fulfilment are in place and already working on it. Everything is possible.

- You are the power creator of your life experiences – Know your power. Your knowing is power...don't waiver.

- Know is it done – you are the master creator of your life. If you decide it is so – then it is so.

Do Things that Help you Feel Wealthy & Prosperous

- Attracting wealth is noticing things that make us feel wealthy and *doing more of those*.

- Don't discount the little wealth things that actually make us feel really rich, in the moment, right here today.

- Notice the things that make you feel wealthy on a daily basis - and schedule them in - **make them a priority**.

- These will be things that that speak *to your heart*. Wealth is very personal. So, please take the time to identify those experiences that speak to you and that are unique to you and do more of them.

Attract by Telling Your New Wealth Story

We all have a wealth story we tell about ourselves to ourselves...usually it is more of a scarcity story. This is your opportunity to write your wealth story the way you want it...and then of course feelize it! Here you are giving yourself permission to write your story; from a no limitation, all things are possible place. Let this be a free flow of ideas, desires and won't-it-be-great-when. This will plant the seeds of the wealth consciousness you are creating.

This is what I want my new wealth story to be...

Attract by Creating a Wealth Persona

Sometimes it is easier for us to imagine wealth for someone else. We can see it for them, but not for us. So, what we are going to do here is create a wealthy character - your wealth persona - that is all of the things that you desire to be, do and have. Create a character that has all the qualities, capabilities and experiences of Big-W*ealthy-You,* the wealthy person you envision. Then practice getting into the feeling-place of your character. The power of this is you get to write the character and be the character you want. Really bring your character to life and really become it and walk in the world like Big-Wealthy-You! How are you feeling throughout the day? What are you doing? How are you talking with your friends?

What would my wealth persona act like? Speak like? Look like? Try? Let go of? Enjoy?

Journal Reflection

Date:

NUGGET I WANT TO REMEMBER

- Clarify what you want – what do I want to FEEL? How does prosperity FEEL? (You might want to start with what you don't want and flip it to what you do…)

- How can I vibrate aligned to prosperity? What will I think? How will I speak? How can I vibrate as prosperity today?

Journal Reflection   Date:

- What doubt might creep in, that I am going to catch and notice, and say "no thank you."

- How am I going to remind myself that my desire is a done deal? How does my heart feel?

POST-PRACTICE
Journal about how you are feeling after the session practice. Be as detailed and specific as you can.

PHYSICALLY (note any changes and insights)

EMOTIONALLY

MENTALLY

OVERAL VITALITY (note any insights)

ONE WORD (how you feel):

PROSPERITY INSIGHTS

Journal about any insights you received in connection with your prosperity thinking and feeling

IMPORTANT NEW AWARENESSES AND IDEAS

NOTEWORTHY (message to yourself)

KEY NUGGET (an important understanding you will take from this)

ONE WORD (how you feel about prosperity now)

ALLOW

- Allowing is cultivating a felt-sense of receptivity to the ever-present Wealth-Energy.

- It is developing our ability to receive and enjoy in grace and ease.

- We learn to allow what we desire to flow to us and we allow others to be who they are, as they are.

- Allowing is a state of being where our mental, emotional and physical resistance is lowered so the Wealth-Energy flows freely through us, as it naturally does - and we get to experience it.

- In this section, you will play with noticing what allowing & truly receiving feels like to you

Allowing is receiving

- Many of us have a hard time with the idea of receiving and allowing ourselves the pleasure of receiving free and clear.

- One of the best examples of the give and take process of life is breathing. We breath in, we receive, we breathe out, we share and give of ourselves. Each moment, we are in this wonderful effortless giving and receiving dance with life.

Allowing in a choice

- Allowing is often the step that is most difficult for many of us to grasp because it asks us to believe, trust and know that prosperity is there for us to receive.

- Allowing is about *believing* **in** the wealth of the universe, *trusting* that it is there for us unconditionally and *knowing* that we have it, so we can be excited and enthusiastic for it to show up in an infinite number of ways for us to receive.

- Allowing is not about doing more. "Doing more" is not necessary. Receiving is not a doing.

Allowing Fosters Fulfillment

If you ask – but cannot receive,

If you create, but cannot allow yourself to have your creation,

If you seek but do not allow yourself to find,

You are only experiencing part of the fulfillment process.

Cultivate a felt-sense of Ease, Flow and Non-Resistance

- Flow is the feeling that things are moving along as smoothly – with no resistance, fears, doubts or worries.

- Flow is shifting our energy from one of pushing and difficult effort, to following synchronicity - acting on our inspirations, honoring unexpected coincidences and paying attention to opportunities that present themselves.

- Ease is where things that seemed difficult become a magical smooth fulfillment.

- Non-Resistance is a release of doubt, fear and worry. It is knowing all is well and all will be well. True relaxation.

What you Desire – Desires you!

- Know your wealth is here. And it desires you.

- *To believe that what you desire - desires you back can be an amazing new revelation.* **Know it is already yours – and wants you too.**

The Power of Yoga Nidra

- Yoga Nidra, or yoga sleep, is a powerful guided practice allowing you to get into a state of deep relaxation.

- It is profoundly healing and transformative and increases your sensitivity to prana and purifies your subtle body.

- Yoga Nidra puts you in a glorious state of allowing. Because when the body is relaxed and the mind is quiet – allowing happens.

Write a Thank you Note for what you are going to receive

Thank you notes are fun to write because they come from a place of feeling like you are so happy to **have received a gift** or had a wonderful time. Thank you notes let us relive the experience we had and make note of it to the person with whom we shared it.

So, now you are going to write a thank you note for what you are going to receive. Write a note to *WUW Unlimited Wealth* (or you pick something/someone that feels good to you) and thank it for all the great experiences you just had; like your finances upgrading, your body feeling great, your relationships blossoming, and feeling light-hearted and free.

The key is to write the note from the place that it has *already happened* and you feel just great about it. Then re-read and re-feel the thank you note every day for 2 weeks and see how this feeling of, "Oh, thank you, thank you, thank you" makes you feel amazing.

Just a Note To Say Thank You So Very Much!

Journal Reflection   Date:

NUGGET I WANT TO REMEMBER

- What does allow or allowing mean to me? More importantly – how does it feel?

- What would it mean to me, if I really embraced the idea that "What I desire, desires me"?

Asana Practice: Journal Reflection   Date:

POST-PRACTICE
Journal about how you are feeling after the session practice. Be as detailed and specific as you can.

PHYSICALLY (note any changes and insights)

EMOTIONALLY

MENTALLY

OVERAL VITALITY (note any insights)

ONE WORD (how you feel):

PROSPERITY INSIGHTS

Journal about any insights you received in connection with your prosperity thinking and feeling

IMPORTANT NEW AWARENESSES AND IDEAS

NOTEWORTHY (message to yourself)

KEY NUGGET (an important understanding you will take from this)

ONE WORD (how you feel about prosperity now)

SESSION 8: FLOW

FLOW

FLOW

Flow is the experience of your prosperity and well-being – being allowed to FLOW through you

- You are a conduit for the prosperity of prana to flow

- Flow is where alignment meets allowing and you experience the fullness of living

- Flow is to prosper, to thrive, to expand

- Your worthiness is never in doubt

Flow is to experience your Eternal Connection to the Divine that is <u>Unbroken</u>

- Ever available

- Always loving and sharing

- Forever with you

- Never ending

- Always flowing - Steady and continuous prana

Flow is not a doing

- Flow is enjoying the moment-to-moment aliveness

- Flow is not about next - it is feeling the continuous stream of aliveness in this present moment, without the notion of waiting for "being ready" or "earning" or any of the future thoughts we have about prosperity.

- It is not trying to reach anywhere – prosperity of life is already here

- No effort is needed to be – there is no special way to be

- You notice and experience the aliveness flowing through you – vibrating you – enlivening you – prana-ing you

Be welcoming of your prosperity

- Open your heart to love – reconnect with that felt-sense of welcoming where your heart is open and your mind is at ease – welcoming life to flow through you.

- Free yourself to be free

- Flow in divine-loving-partnership with the magical mystery of life

- Feel the abundant flow of living free of resistance, resentment or regret

Cultivate the felt-sense of ease and flow

Do things that feel flowy, like:

- Yoga asana flows from one pose to another can give you a sense of flow

- Driving down the highway with no traffic

- Enjoying the breeze, riding a bike, sailing gives the felt-sense of flow

- Walking in Nature

- Noticing the song of a flower

Be open to Mystery

- When you are in flow, life is an adventure because you are in the present moment – being moved by the flow of the Unlimited moving though you – as you.

- This means unexpected ideas, synchronicities and unplanned experiences are flowing to you to move you toward your desires.

- This takes a bit of trust, but when you are aligned and in flow you feel guided and supported. You know you are loved and can relax into the prosperity of the unknown. Enjoy.

Everything is already ok

"Everything is already OK. The notion strikes us as radical and it surely is. What it means is that in our essential nature, we are already fully awake and enlightened; it means that God is available to us fully in the moment, simply because God is our true nature. We simply have to stop resisting it. There is no distance to travel, nothing special that we have to do to earn God. It is a "done deal".

- Stephen Cope in Meditations from the Mat

ENJOY! ENJOY! ENJOY!

Namaste

Journal Reflection	**Date:**

NUGGET I WANT TO REMEMBER

- What is flow to me? How does it feel?

- What are things/experiences I do that give me that felt sense of flow?

- If I were to allow myself to live my life in flow – what would I do more of, what would I let go of, what would I do less of?

Journal Reflection	Date:

- Am I open to mystery and the unexpected? What if I let down my guard or did not control? How would that feel?

- Can I allow life to flow with me, through me and around me freely? Why or Why not?

- What is different (in me and around me) now that I have taken this journey?

Journal Reflection   Date:

- What is my definition of prosperity now? As I look back over my journal entries and my practice reflections ...what am I noticing?

Asana Practice: Journal Reflection   Date:

POST-PRACTICE
Journal about how you are feeling after the session practice. Be as detailed and specific as you can.

PHYSICALLY (note any changes and insights)

EMOTIONALLY

MENTALLY

OVERAL VITALITY (note any insights)

ONE WORD (how you feel):

PROSPERITY INSIGHTS
Journal about any insights you received in connection with your prosperity thinking and feeling

IMPORTANT NEW AWARENESSES AND IDEAS

NOTEWORTHY (message to yourself)

KEY NUGGET (an important understanding you will take from this)

ONE WORD (how you feel about prosperity now)

About Author: Tricia Fiske

Author, Tricia Fiske, BA, E-RYT 500, YACEP®, **Certified ParaYoga® Level III & Certified Four Desires Trainer,** is a former corporate executive who began teaching yoga in 1999. She has been studying exclusively with ParaYoga® founder Rod Stryker since 2000, and was one of the first Level III certified teachers in this rigorous training.

She is the co-author of **From Alignment to Enlightenment: Using Props to Achieve Stability and Ease in Yoga Poses**

As primary faculty at Prairie Yoga in Lisle, Illinois, Tricia is a teacher of teachers, one of the most respected in the Midwest. She was one of the first yoga teachers in the Western suburbs of Chicago and has trained and influenced a generation of yoga students and teachers. A longtime faculty member at the College of DuPage, she mentors yoga teachers, conducts workshops, and recently presented at the Sedona Yoga Festival.

For more information on Tricia, visit her website:

www.TriciaFiske.com

and follow her on Facebook.

About Author: Laurie LaMantia

Author, **Laurie LaMantia,** is a successful entrepreneur, professor and artist who shares her wisdom about developing wealth consciousness to her many students. She has been developing her wealth consciousness from a very young age and has learned both how to allow wealth and repel it.

She has been a student and teacher of yoga for over 20 years.

She also teaches Leadership, Creativity in Business and Entrepreneurship at DePaul University's School of Business. She is the co-author of **Breakthrough Teams for Breakneck Times,** a book on unlocking the genius of collaboration.

And the author of **Effortless Wealth: A Guide for developing your wealth consciousness.**

As the marketing and sales director of her manufacturing company, she sees the opportunity daily to foster wealth and prosperity in the company, which is an exploration in deeply held business agreements about prosperity.

Laurie is the Chief Prosperity Officer for The Abundance Center. She has an MBA from Northwestern Kellogg School of Management, an MS- IOE from University of Michigan and bachelors in Electronic Engineering from DeVry.

For more wealth resources please visit:

www.TheAbundanceCenter.com

Remember...live long and know you are always prospering

www.ingramcontent.com/pod-product-compliance
Lightning Source LLC
Chambersburg PA
CBHW062049090426
42740CB00016B/3075